Local Sanctuary

Dylan Punke

Copyright © 2011 Dylan Punke

All rights reserved.

ISBN: 1463506031
ISBN-13: 978-1463506032

To those with foresight to preserve. To those who cultivate for generations they will never know.

Life has allowed me the luxury of travel since I can remember. If I am not in movement, I am often dreaming about the possibility of movement. My mind often dreams of exotic and unknown territories, quite alluring and distracting. From the Grand Canyon to the mighty Amazon River, Angel Falls to the Himalayas, the Pyramids to the Great Wall; there is a ceaseless tempt. Recently my journey of being on the road hasn't brought me to these international treasures but instead to a quiet local nature preserve. This preserve is often overlooked, rarely on a map, and never in a guidebook, but is still tended by dedicated hands and persevering minds.

Rediscovering and exploring this preserve, I am learning a lesson that I have resisted; to love the land that is beneath my feet. I thought I knew this land that I grew tall in but I have barely scratched the surface. Growth occurs from the preserve's allowance of intimate pondering, meditation, reflection, and recreation that has long been hidden by ambitious pursuits. Upon every entry, it renews, regenerates, and reestablishes the natural connection that is so often deprived. A grounding yet paradoxically uplifting reality emerges, instead of an alluring and distracting dream. I can enter with the foggiest of minds and leave with clearness that once seemed unreachable.

The tranquility found in the woods and the flow of the river has taught me to reconsider beauty. I am slowly understanding that beauty is not only reflected in the natural world, but we as humans being a part of the natural world, are capable of having that beauty illuminate within. I am seeing that beauty is everywhere and it is not necessary to roam the earth to find such. The following photographs are my attempt at capturing some of this beauty from my personal journey, but are not intended to replace the physical realm of being in its presence.

It is not my hope that this particular place is flocked to in great numbers or that the photographs in it are attempted to be replicated. I hope that you are inspired to stop in your own lands to gain your own fresh approach and appreciate that which is in front of you. To be willing to re-envision what has patiently been waiting all along underneath your feet and within you. Much as it is rare to daily worship in the grandest of temples it is also rare to daily trek in the world's international treasures. So whether it be a sprawling oasis in the middle of plowed earth or the tiniest of parks dwarfed by urban density, I hope you find your own Local Sanctuary.

Winter Gate

Prairie Snow

Snowy Stream

Grayish Winter

Hillside Nudes

Snowy Dance

Winter Vines

Winter, Y

Winter Walk

Tiered Powder

Lowland Winter

Unbeaten Path

Refuge

Mackinaw

Chilly Creek

Winter Tributary

Winter Cast

Aura

Wintry Dusk

Fallen Giant

Raised Branches

Cool Leaf

Lighting Pines

Soft Winter Blues

Winter Warmth

Winter Crossing

Winter Clearing

Prairie & Fence

Quiet Neighbors

Impression

Vertical Tangent

Dormant Blues

Golden Grass

Leanings

Assemblage

Yellow Prairie I

Yellow Prairie II

Legacy

Crossing Barren Trees

Out of Shell

From Above

Majestic

Distant Kin

Sprouting Lineage

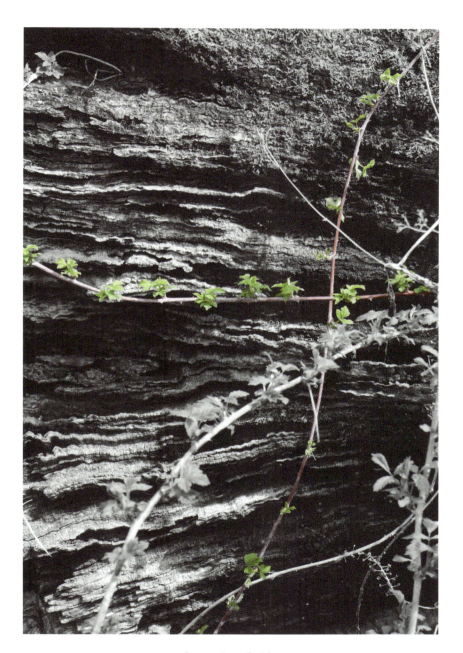

Crossing Paths

Creek Crossing

Bridge to Beauty

Spring Creek

Spring Greeting

Blue Comfort

Lowland Blues

Rooted Bluebells

Enchant

Shaded Blues

Intimate Virginia

Spring Beauty

Centrifugal Burst

Abuzz

Glimmer

Small Friends

Quiet Gatherings

Muted Beauty

Guarded Beauty

Prairie Cone

Pollen Buzz

Upwards

Thorns

Faux Summer Raindrops

Small Ideas

Yellow Tufts

Solo Journey

Crimson Base

Thistle

Parkland

Delicate Path

Parkland Trail

Convert

River Leaf

Swift

Meander

Flow

Mackinaw Fall Reflection

Faint Fall

Autumn

Elevated Autumn

Aglow

Radiance

Autumn Oak

Fall Fence

Autumn Morning

Waft

Fall

Let Go

Barrenness

Path Keepers

Untitled

Root Veins

Leaf and Needles

Battered Leaf

In Light

The creation of this book stems from no expertise on the subjects contained within. My hands never interacted directly with its foresight of preservation, reclamation of lands, or reseeding of forgotten inhabitants. All of the photographs were taken in a common location that was easily and often reached by a rickety old bicycle.

Dylan Punke

Dylan Punke is a self-learning photographer from the Bloomington-Normal area of Illinois. The works contained in Local Sanctuary and other works by Dylan can be found at his website:

www.dep-artgallery.com

All content in this work is copyrighted © Dylan Punke

Made in the USA
Charleston, SC
02 July 2011